Albert Einstein
A Life of Genius

written by Elizabeth MacLeod

Kids Can Press

With much love to my favorite Einstein and nephew, Jack

Consultant: Prof. Allan Griffin, Department of Physics, University of Toronto, Toronto, Ontario, Canada

Acknowledgments

Many, many thanks to Professor Allan Griffin for his patience and his interest in this book. I so appreciate the time he spent reviewing the pages and making sure both the facts about Albert and the physics were correct. I'm very grateful for all of his assistance.

Thanks also to Karen Powers for another terrific design, and for all the many other things she did to make this book possible. I really appreciate her willingness to go far beyond the call of duty to add the details that make this series of books look so terrific.

I'm very grateful to Patricia Buckley for her hard work, persistence and creativity in obtaining the photos for this book. Barbara Spurll's illustrations of Albert look terrific and add so much.

Many thanks to the entire Kids Can Press team, including Rivka Cranley and Valerie Hussey. Very special thanks, as ever, to Val Wyatt, for her wonderful editing and friendship. I so appreciate her hard work, care, sense of humor and style. Her patience and creativity are inspiring.

Thanks always to my dad and to John and Douglas. And of course much love and gratitude to Paul who helped me with this book, and assists me with all my writing in more ways than he knows.

Text © 2003 Elizabeth MacLeod
Illustrations of Einstein © 2003 Barbara Spurll

All rights reserved. No part of this publication may be reproduced, stored in a retrieval system or transmitted, in any form or by any means, without the prior written permission of Kids Can Press Ltd. or, in case of photocopying or other reprographic copying, a license from CANCOPY (Canadian Copyright Licensing Agency), 1 Yonge Street, Suite 1900, Toronto, ON, M5E 1E5.

Kids Can Press acknowledges the financial support of the Ontario Arts Council, the Canada Council for the Arts and the Government of Canada, through the BPIDP, for our publishing activity.

Published in Canada by
Kids Can Press Ltd.
29 Birch Avenue
Toronto, ON M4V 1E2

Published in the U.S. by
Kids Can Press Ltd.
2250 Military Road
Tonawanda, NY 14150

www.kidscanpress.com

Edited by Valerie Wyatt
Designed by Karen Powers
Printed in Hong Kong, China.

The hardcover edition of this book is smyth sewn casebound.
The paperback edition of this book is limp sewn with a drawn-on cover.

CM 03 0 9 8 7 6 5 4 3 2 1
CM PA 03 0 9 8 7 6 5 4 3 2 1

National Library of Canada Cataloguing in Publication Data

MacLeod, Elizabeth
    Albert Einstein : a life of genius / Elizabeth MacLeod.

Includes index.

ISBN 1-55337-396-0 (bound).   ISBN 1-55337-397-9 (pbk.)

1. Einstein, Albert, 1879–1955 — Juvenile literature. 2. Physicists — Biography — Juvenile literature. I. Title.

QC16.E5M25 2003   j530'.092   C2002-903078-1

Photo credits

Every reasonable effort has been made to trace ownership of and give accurate credit to copyrighted material. Information that would enable the publisher to correct any discrepancies in future editions would be appreciated.

Abbreviations
t = top; b = bottom; c = center; l = left; r = right

American Institute of Physics/Emilio Segrè Visual Archives: 16(t), 17(t), 21(cl), 24(t), 25(l); **Frank Baldaserra:** back cover (tl), 12(b), 17(bl), 23(cr); **Courtesy University of Bern:** 15(br); **Bettmann/Corbis/Magma:** front cover (r), 4(t), 21(t), 21(b); **Bibliothéque Nationale Suisse:** 8, 9(tl); **Courtesy Bulletin of the Atomic Scientists:** 29(tr); **Reproduced with permission California Institute of Technology:** 5(tl), 9(bl), 27(t); **Comstock Royalty Free:** 5(tl), 6(b); **ETH-Bibliothek:** 1, 9(tr), 17(c, br); **Reproduced with permission of The Huntingdon Library,** San Marino, California: back cover, 3(br), 19(t); **Courtesy of the Archives of the Institute for Advanced Study:** back cover (tr), 26(b), 28; **Used with permission of Kraft Canada Inc., under license from Kraft Foods Schweiz AG:** 9(br), 15(tr); **Library of Congress:** 10(t,b), 27(c); **Mary Lea Shane Archives of the Lick Observatory:** 19(b); **Lotte Jacobi Archives/University of New Hampshire:** 3(bl), 6(t), 13(b), 14, 15(bl), 18(b), 20, 29(bl); **NASA:** front cover (l), 3(c), 11(b), 12(t), 13(l), 29(br); **National Archives of Canada/PAC-928:** 18(t); **Courtesy Museum of New Mexico/Photo by El Tovar Studio/38193:** 23(b); **Copyright © The Nobel Foundation:** 21(cr); **Ponopresse:** 15(tl); **Collections of the Historical Society of Princeton:** 23(cl); **Franklin D. Roosevelt Library:** 25(b); **Edgar Fahs Smith Collection/University of Pennsylvania Library:** 11(cl); **Stadtarchiv Ulm:** back cover (lc), 3(t), 7(t), 7(b); **Toronto Reference Library:** 27(b); **United States Archives and Holocaust Museum/05459:** 22; **United States Archives and Holocaust Museum/68984:** 23(t); **United States Immigration and Naturalization Service:** 24(b); **United States National Archives:** front cover (c), 5(b), 25(r); **Reprinted with permission of Dr. S.F. Witelson from The Lancet, 1999, 353, 2149-2153:** 29(tl).

Kids Can Press is a **Corus**™ Entertainment company

$E=mc^2$

Contents

felde eine Deviation erfahren.
Grav. Feld
Lichtstrahl

Am Sonnenrande müsste diese Ablenkung
0,84" betragen und wie $\frac{1}{R}$ abnehmen
$(R = \text{Entfernung vom Sonnen- Mittelpunkt})$.

0,84"

Sonne

Es wäre deshalb von grösstem

Meet Albert Einstein

In this photo, taken on his 72nd birthday, Albert hammed it up for the camera.

Sure, science is serious, but you can't be serious all the time.

Ask people to name a scientist and they'll probably all say the same thing — Albert Einstein. With his bushy white hair, droopy moustache and rumpled clothes, he looks like everyone's image of an absentminded scientist.

Albert *was* absentminded but he was also brilliant. He's famous for his discoveries about time, light and gravity and how they affect the universe. His theories changed the world of physics — the study of matter (things) and energy and how they interact. He also showed how everything moves, from the tiniest particles to the largest planets. Albert was what's known as a theoretical physicist — he used math to explain what he and other scientists observed in the world around them.

Some scientists prefer the lab to the real world, but Albert wasn't one of them. Physics filled his mind most of the time — however he also tried to be part of what was going on around him. He felt that scientists have to be responsible for their work and how it affects people. World peace was also very important to him, and he traveled the world talking to people about it.

While Albert was serious about science and the importance of peace, he still liked to have fun. He loved playing his violin and munching on cookies. Even when he was old, he'd play with kids he met on his walk to work, sometimes joining in their water-pistol fights.

Was Albert a genius, as many people have claimed? What was he like to live with? How did he figure out so much about the world, more than anyone else has and probably ever will?

Einstein is German for "one stone." Thanks to Albert's incredible accomplishments, Einstein now means genius in any language.

One of Albert's theories said that speed makes time slow down. Now that super-precise clocks can measure time in nanoseconds (billionths of a second), scientists have found that Albert was right.

All his life Albert liked hiking, sailing and biking. He never learned to drive — he thought it was too complicated.

Albert was so famous that people wanted to hear what he had to say about almost any subject. He often spoke about the importance of world peace.

"It's not that I'm so smart, it's just that I stay with problems longer."
— Albert

Early thinking

When Albert first saw his baby sister, he asked, "Where are her wheels?" He thought Maria — he always called her Maja — was some kind of toy.

When Albert was about four, his father gave him a compass. It fascinated Albert — why did its needle always point north? All his life Albert was curious about how the world works and remembered this compass.

"Much too fat! Much too fat," Albert's grandmother cried when she first saw him. What an ugly baby! Albert was tubby with a huge, misshapen head. In a few months his weight was normal, but the back of his skull never lost its odd shape.

Hermann and Pauline Einstein worried about their son. Until he was three, he hardly talked. What his parents didn't know was that Albert had decided he wouldn't speak until he could talk in whole sentences.

Albert had a good sense of humor — and a bad temper. He didn't much like other kids, preferring to play the violin alone. School — especially math — was a breeze, but he hated it. It was too strict. Albert didn't like memorizing, and he wanted to *ask* questions, not answer them. No wonder his classmates called him "Biedermeier," which means something like today's "nerd." Albert's lessons continued outside of school — his family was Jewish and Albert received religious instruction at home.

When Albert was 15, his father's electric business in Munich, Germany, failed and the family moved to Milan, Italy — except for Albert. He stuck it out in Munich for six months on his own before dropping out of school to join his family. In Milan, he lounged around for half a year, then his parents announced it was time for him to begin studying again.

Albert decided to attend the famous Swiss Federal Institute of Technology in Zurich, Switzerland. He studied hard for the Institute's entrance exam. The math and physics sections were easy, but he did so badly in French, chemistry and biology — he couldn't care less about them — that he failed the exam. He had to study for another year before he made it into the Institute.

In 1896, at the age of 17, Albert began a four-year course to teach math and physics. But school bored him, so he skipped lectures and talked back to his professors. Luckily he had two good friends who shared their notes with him. Even in labs he didn't listen to his professors. Because of this, one of his experiments blew up and he needed stitches in his hand.

After graduation Albert wanted to work at the Institute. But he'd been so rude to his teachers that none of them would help him. He was forced to teach wherever he could, at high schools or as a substitute teacher. Albert liked teaching but he wanted to keep studying physics at university. Would he ever get the chance again?

I was born in Ulm, Germany, a town famous for having the world's tallest church steeple.

Here are some of the cities in Europe where Albert lived.

Albert is about 10 in this school photo. He did well only in math and Latin. He liked the fact that Latin grammar is logical.

Berlin

GERMANY

Prague
CZECH
REPUBLIC

Ulm
Munich

Bern
Zurich

SWITZERLAND

Milan

ITALY

A university student who was a friend of the family and much older than Albert liked discussing math with him. However, the student soon found that Albert knew far more than he did.

"You are a very clever boy, Einstein, an extremely clever boy, but you have one great fault: you never let yourself be told anything."
— one of Albert's teachers

$$x = \frac{-b \pm \sqrt{b^2 - 4ac}}{2a}$$

Patent for success

Albert gave Mileva the nickname Doxerl, which means "little doll." Johonzel, or Johnnie, was Mileva's nickname for Albert.

"I'm so lucky to have found you, a creature who is my equal, and who is strong and independent as I am. I feel alone with everyone except you."
— Albert, writing to Mileva

Albert finally landed a permanent job — but it had nothing to do with physics. Instead, a friend's father got him work at the patent office in Bern, Switzerland. Albert's job was to study the descriptions that inventors sent in and decide if their inventions were new and deserved patents.

Sometimes when inventors applied for patents they wrote confusing descriptions of their work. Albert had to rewrite them, which taught him how to say things clearly. That skill would come in handy later when he was writing up his own theories.

Albert liked his work and he was good at it. A lot of the inventions involved electricity, and thanks to his father's electrical business, he had a head start. Albert was also good at imagining what the inventors were describing, perhaps because he'd had lots of practice working things out mentally. Ever since he was young, he'd performed what he called "thought experiments," testing theories and experiments in his mind. He would use this skill all his life.

Long hours at the patent office meant that Albert had to fit in his physics experiments when he could. And he had something else to take up his time. He'd fallen in love with Mileva Maric, one of the classmates who'd lent him notes back at the Institute. In the late 1800s it was unusual for a woman to attend university, especially to study science, but Mileva was brilliant at physics and math.

Mileva and Albert had a daughter in 1902. Because they weren't married, they gave up Lieserl for adoption. No one knows what happened to her. The couple was married later that year. Even on their wedding day, Albert had his mind on other things — and forgot the key to their apartment.

If work was slow at the patent office, Albert scribbled equations on paper he kept in his desk drawer — he called it his physics department. Mileva and Albert had another baby in 1904, whom they named Hans Albert (they called him Albertli). Even when Albert took his son out for a walk, he carried a notepad so that he could write down his ideas.

His thinking paid off. In 1904 Albert wrote three articles for a major German science journal (magazine) and began to make a name for himself. But no one knew that, in less than a year, Albert would change the world of physics.

This is where Albert and Mileva lived in Bern. Late into the night and on his days off, Albert would work on physics, ignoring everything around him. If Mileva went away for a few days, she'd come back to find Albert surrounded by a mess of papers and dirty dishes.

Albert (right) liked to meet with Konrad Habicht (left) and Maurice Solovine to hike and discuss the latest scientific research. The friends decided their little trio should have a big important name so they chose Olympia Academy — in Greek legends, Olympia was the home of the gods.

Albert was happy at the patent office — he liked inventors and their creations, and he got along well with the people in his office.

I worked on many patents, including this one. A patent is a legal document that keeps people from copying an inventor's creation.

SCHWEIZ EIDGENO

EIDGEN. AMT FÜR

PATENTSCHRIFT

708

29. März 1909, 5 Uhr p.

HAUPTPATENT

CHOCOLADE-FABRIK TOBLER & Co. A. G. Be

Verfahren zur Herstellung einer neuartigen Schokolade.

Physics before Albert

Galileo Galilei thought out experiments in his mind — just as Albert Einstein would do centuries later.

James Maxwell knew a lot about light, electricity and magnetism. He even figured out that Saturn's rings must be made of small particles. Scientists had to wait until the *Voyager* spacecrafts cruised by Saturn in the 1980s to show that Maxwell was right.

Long before Albert was born, people were interested in physics — the study of matter and energy and how they interact. Scientists were already using what they knew about physics, such as how things move on Earth, to figure out more about the motions of the Sun and planets.

For thousands of years, people thought that Earth was the center of the universe and everything revolved around it. Then, in 1543, Nicolaus Copernicus, a Polish astronomer, published his theory on how the planets, including Earth, orbit around the Sun.

The next big breakthrough in physics came from Galileo Galilei, an Italian mathematician. In the 1600s Galileo showed that Copernicus was probably right. Galileo also had theories about how things move on Earth and about gravity. He dropped things off the Leaning Tower of Pisa just to see which fell faster. He discovered that all objects fall at the same rate, no matter what they weigh.

Then physics took a giant leap forward. In 1687 Sir Isaac Newton explained how all objects in the universe — even the planets — move. His laws and theories used math and also made predictions, for the first time. Scientists still consider Newton the most famous physicist ever.

Next physicists tackled magnetism and electricity. In 1865 James Maxwell, a Scottish physicist, developed the math to describe electric and magnetic fields and how they affect each other. Then Maxwell realized that they're part of the same thing — electromagnetism.

Maxwell produced the first complete theory about what light is and how fast it moves. But scientists still didn't know *how* light moves. Outer space is empty so there's nothing to carry the light waves along. Maxwell and others thought light moved through a fluid called ether, which filled all space.

Albert Michelson and Edward Morley thought Maxwell was right, and in 1887 the two American physicists tested for ether by looking for changes in the speed of light. But they found no changes. They proved that light always moves at the same speed — Albert would base his theory of relativity (see page 12) on this.

That's about how much scientists knew about physics around the time Albert Einstein began studying. But he was about to shake up the world of physics with a whole new explanation of how things move.

When English physicist Sir Isaac Newton saw an apple fall from a tree in 1666, it made him wonder why things fall down. Why don't they fall up or sideways? Questions like this helped him discover and name "gravity" and figure out the laws about how gravity works.

Astronomy today had its beginnings in the ideas of Nicolaus Copernicus. Amazingly, Copernicus didn't even have a telescope — it hadn't yet been invented.

"Anyone who has never made a mistake has never tried anything new." — Albert

I had this portrait of Sir Isaac Newton hanging in my office for many years.

Albert Michelson and Edward Morley measured the speed of light when it travels in the same direction as Earth, as well as in the opposite direction. To their surprise, light's speed was always constant.

Albert's miracle year

The *Cassini* spacecraft, launched in 1997, is one of the largest, heaviest and most complex spacecraft ever. Albert's special theory of relativity is the basis of the technology used.

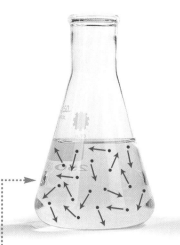

One of Albert's papers explained the random movement of small, lightweight particles in a liquid, such as dust particles in water. Scientists call this Brownian motion and use Albert's theory to explain many random movements or events.

After spending all day, six days a week, at the patent office, Albert went home and wrestled with his thought experiments long into the night. He often ignored Mileva and Hans Albert because his head was bursting with new ideas and theories to explain how the universe works.

Albert's ideas came pouring out in 1905, when he had four articles published in Germany's most important physics journal. Each was probably good enough to win physics' top award, the Nobel prize. Albert published all four in one year.

One of Albert's papers gave the first convincing evidence for the existence of atoms and molecules. Another paper was about light waves. Physicists already knew that light is a form of energy made of tiny particles, or "quanta." (The study of how these light quanta behave is part of quantum physics.) Albert argued that light travels both as a particle *and* a wave — an amazing new idea.

But by far the most famous paper made people think of time and space differently. Newton had said that time and distance are constant — a minute is always a minute long and a kilometer (or mile) is always the same length. He also said that mass (the amount of matter in an object — on Earth, it's related to the object's weight) never changes either. But Albert realized all three — time, distance and mass — can change, depending on how fast you are moving. He called this paper the "Special Theory of Relativity."

What's relativity? Have you ever noticed when you're sitting in a smoothly moving car it seems as if the buildings outside are moving and you're sitting still? They *are* moving, compared with, or *relative* to, you. Albert included the word "special" in the title of his theory because it's only correct in one special case when objects are moving at a constant speed.

After Albert had sent off his paper about the special theory of relativity, he thought about it some more. He proved that energy (E) and mass (m) are different forms of the same thing and he figured out how they're linked — that's where his famous equation $E = mc^2$ comes from (the letter c stands for the speed of light).

It's hard to follow some of Albert's ideas because they don't affect most people's lives. You can't zoom around at light speed, so you don't notice changes in how quickly time is passing. But scientists working on space travel or nuclear reactors today depend on Albert's equations.

"… the years of anxious searching in the dark, with their intense longing, their alternations of confidence and exhaustion and the final emergence into the light — only those who have experienced it can understand it." — Albert

The speed of light is represented by the letter c — it stands for the Latin word for speed, celeritas.

$$E = mc^2$$

The most famous equation in physics says that the energy (E) in an object is equal to its mass (m) multiplied by the speed of light (c), then multiplied by the speed of light again.

Albert was able to publish his four incredible papers in just one year because he'd been thinking about them for years and discussing them with Mileva and friends.

Mercury's orbit had long puzzled scientists. Newton couldn't explain it, and neither could Albert's special theory of relativity. But, as he often did, Albert kept mulling over his theory. He later developed his general theory of relativity (see page 19), which *did* explain Mercury's motion.

Professor Einstein

"If A = success, then the formula is A = X + Y + Z, where X is 'work,' Y is 'play,' and Z is 'keep your mouth shut.'"

— Albert

Max Planck was world famous because of his theory about light quanta. He wrote to Albert about Albert's theory of relativity. Albert was pleased that such a brilliant scientist had noticed his work.

Not everyone accepted Albert's theories right away. They were difficult to understand and challenged what scientists had believed for hundreds of years. Besides, Albert was only 26 — how could he know more about physics than much older scientists? So nothing changed for Albert. He kept working at the patent office and thinking about physics.

One day at work Albert imagined what it would be like to fall off a roof. He figured you wouldn't feel your weight — until you hit the ground. You'd feel weightless because gravity would accelerate all the molecules in your body at the same speed. Albert called it the "happiest thought of my life," and it was the start of his greatest theory. His special theory of relativity applied only to objects moving at a constant speed, but now Albert thought about what happens when things accelerate, or change their speed.

Albert also kept thinking about quanta (light particles), the subject of one of his famous 1905 papers. In 1900 physicist Max Planck had come up with the theory that light was made up of quanta, but it was Albert who realized the importance of this concept and developed it. He showed how these light quanta (today called photons) could be absorbed by metals.

At last universities began to notice Albert Einstein. Could his dream of teaching and studying physics at a university finally be coming true? The university in Bern, Switzerland, hired him as a kind of private teacher. It wasn't much of a job and the pay was bad, but Albert knew it was the first step toward becoming a professor.

And it worked. In 1909 the University of Zurich in Switzerland finally appointed him professor of theoretical physics. Fancy titles didn't impress Albert. He was as friendly to janitors as he was to the most important professors. That same year he and many world-famous scientists were honored by Switzerland's University of Geneva. Everyone was well dressed in special robes — except Albert. He wore an ordinary suit and straw hat. Appearances didn't matter to him.

In 1910 Albert and Mileva had another son, Eduard. They called him Tete or Tetel. But life was not happy in the Einstein home. Mileva wanted more time with Albert and wanted to help with his work. She was good at physics and math, too. Albert saw things differently — he wanted Mileva to take over the jobs around the house. After all, he had thinking to do.

Here is Albert's wife, Mileva, with their two sons, Eduard (left) and Hans Albert. When it was Albert's turn to babysit, he'd hold baby Eduard with his left hand while writing out equations with his right *and* talking to Hans Albert.

I approved the patent for the mold used to make the Toblerone chocolate bar.

In 1909 Albert quit the patent office. His boss couldn't understand why he would leave such a good job. Obviously, his boss wasn't a scientist.

Albert liked living in Bern, Switzerland, and was happy to be teaching at the university there (below), but he wasn't a great professor. Most students simply couldn't keep up with him.

On the brink

Albert said that Marie Curie was "the only person not corrupted by fame."

Marie Curie and I became good friends. We even took our children on a holiday together.

Hans Albert knew his father worked hard, but he wasn't really sure that Albert's work made much sense. So one day when Hans Albert was about eight, he took Albert aside and said, "Father, we're alone, nobody can see or hear us. Now you can tell me — is this relativity story all bunk?"

Albert's son may have had doubts about his work, but other people didn't. The university in Prague, Czech Republic, offered Albert twice as much money as he was making in Zurich, so the Einstein family moved there. Albert wanted to make a good first impression and began visiting the other professors to introduce himself. But the visits bored him, so he stopped before he'd met everyone and ended up offending the people he'd missed.

As well as teaching, Albert kept conducting thought experiments and publishing papers. In 1911 his work gained him an invitation to the first Solvay Congress. This gathering of about 20 of the world's most brilliant physicists was a first in the world. Some of their discussions involved a new theory that would bring together relativity, the quantum (a tiny packet of energy) and radioactivity (the ability of some materials to give off particles).

One of the scientists at the Solvay Congress was Marie Curie. She was the most famous woman in science — her work with radioactivity had won her science's highest award, a Nobel prize. The first woman to win a Nobel prize, Marie was also the first person to win this award twice. She and Albert became friends because they were both more interested in science than in fame.

After the Solvay Congress even more universities wanted Albert. In 1912 Zurich University offered him a big raise, so back he went. About a year later, he took yet another new job, this time at the University of Berlin in Germany. But Mileva was very unhappy there and she decided to move back to Zurich with their sons. Albert cried as their train chugged away. He never lived with his family again.

"Only two things are infinite, the universe and human stupidity, and I'm not sure about the former." — Albert

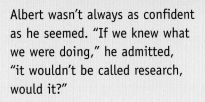

Albert wasn't always as confident as he seemed. "If we knew what we were doing," he admitted, "it wouldn't be called research, would it?"

In this snapshot, taken at the 1911 Solvay Congress, Marie Curie is busy reviewing a paper, while Albert looks on.

University students were welcome to visit Albert in his office any time. He didn't mind interruptions — he told his pupils that he could drop what he was doing and easily pick it up when they left.

The Swiss Federal Institute of Technology in Zurich is often called the ETH, short for its German name Eidgenössische Technische Hochschule. This is its physics institute where Albert worked.

It's all relative

The horrors of war sickened Albert. One of the worst weapons in World War I was poisonous gas. Gas masks gave soldiers a bit of protection.

Albert spent time with his cousin Elsa Löwenthal in Berlin. They fell in love, so he divorced Mileva and married Elsa in 1919. Elsa was very shortsighted and once at a dinner ate a flower arrangement thinking it was a salad!

Albert was miserable. He believed in world peace, but by 1914 World War I was raging across Europe. He also missed his sons. So he threw himself into a physics project he'd been thinking about for 10 years.

He often became so lost in his work that he forgot to eat. Or he'd gulp down cookies or boil an egg in a pot of soup, then eat them both. He eventually collapsed with stomach pains. But he didn't care. He'd finally figured out how to include gravity in his special theory of relativity and finished his greatest work, the "General Theory of Relativity."

The general theory of relativity says that space is warped, or "curved," by objects. Things are pulled toward more massive objects by this curve of space. That's why Earth orbits the Sun.

Albert's theory also says that everything, including light, is affected by gravity. This means that starlight traveling near the Sun should be pulled toward it, following the curve of space near the Sun.

To prove his theory, Albert wanted astronomers to compare a star's position at two different seasons to see if the light coming from it was being bent. If the star seemed to shift in the sky, it would prove that its light had been bent by the Sun's gravity.

But the star could only be photographed when it looked as if it was close to the Sun — that's when its light would pass near enough to the Sun to be bent. And the only time a star appears to be close to the Sun is in the daytime. So how do you photograph a star during the day? Maybe during a solar eclipse, thought Albert, when the sky is dark. By comparing a photo of a star during an eclipse with the same star at a different season, any bending of the light would be easy to see.

Albert had to wait three years for the next solar eclipse. In 1919 British astronomers agreed to take photos and analyze the results. Was Albert right? He waited months for confirmation. Finally a telegram arrived — the photos showed the shift that Albert had calculated.

Albert became world famous. Ordinary people didn't understand his theory, but World War I had just ended and they wanted good news. Albert's successful theory — and the fact German and British scientists had worked together, despite the war — fit the bill. This was the first really new theory about the force of gravity since Newton's original ideas 250 years earlier.

*ass Lichtstrahlen in einem Gravitations-
elde eine Deviation erfahren.*

Grav. Feld

Lichtstrahl

Am Sonnenrande müsste diese Ablenkung

,84" betragen und wie $\frac{1}{R}$ abnehmen

(Entfernung vom Sonnen-Mittelpunkt)

R = Sonnenradius).

0,84"

Sonne

Es wäre deshalb von grösstem
Interesse, bis zu wie grosser Sonnen-
nähe (helle) Fixsterne bei Anwendun
er stärksten Vergrösserungen bei Tag
ohne Sonnenfinsternis) gesehen werd
können.

"I sometimes ask myself why I was the one to develop the theory of relativity. The reason, I think, is that a normal adult never stops to think about problems of space and time. These are things … thought of as a child."

— Albert

Albert had been impatient to have his theory about the effect of gravity on starlight confirmed. As early as 1913 he wrote to the famous American astronomer George Ellery Hale to find out if waiting for the next eclipse was really necessary. Hale told him that it was.

Astronomers journeyed long distances to take the eclipse photos to confirm Albert's theory. Of course he never had any doubts about his theory, but now other physicists and astronomers believed it too.

Albert liked working in Berlin. He had relatives there and his job as a university professor let him do as much research and thinking as he liked.

My Berlin relatives thought I was just a dreamer — until I became a professor at one of the world's top scientific institutions.

Berlin 7/1 04

World-famous scientist

Sailing was one of Albert's favorite hobbies.

I liked sailing because it gave me a chance to get away from people.

World War I was over but conditions in Berlin, where Albert was teaching, were hard. Food was scarce and expensive. There were strikes all over Germany and fighting on the streets as people battled for control.

Albert's fame grew and he won many awards. In 1916, the year he published his general theory of relativity, more than a hundred articles and books were written about it. One science magazine offered $5000 — a lot of money then — for the clearest 3000-word explanation of relativity. Albert didn't enter because he didn't think he could do it.

Albert was becoming more aware of his Jewish roots. Germany had lost the war, and many Germans blamed the Jews for the loss. This angered and worried Albert. In 1921 when he was asked to tour the United States to help raise money for the Hebrew University in Jerusalem, Israel, a school especially for Jews, Albert said yes. While in the United States, he also lectured to packed halls about his theory of relativity.

The trip to the United States was the start of Albert's world travels. During the next few years he visited England, France, Austria, the Czech Republic, South America, Palestine and Spain. Albert and Elsa were in Japan in 1922 when he got word that he'd won the Nobel prize in physics. Albert was pleased but he'd been so sure that he would eventually win this famous prize that he'd already promised the $35 000 prize money to Mileva, to look after their sons.

Even while traveling, Albert made time for physics. He was now trying to find a way to connect the theories of electromagnetism and gravity. He called what he was searching for the "unified field theory." Most physicists thought that it was too difficult to find and that Albert was wasting his time. Albert agreed and yet believed that the work might yield some interesting discoveries. He knew younger theoretical physicists couldn't afford to try and fail but felt he was well established and could risk failure. He also loved to think about difficult problems.

Albert also had a theory about a new kind of ultracold gas called a Bose-Einstein condensate. (Indian physicist Satyendra Nath Bose inspired the idea.) The condensate wasn't created until 1995. One day it could lead to a new type of technology.

The traveling and work were too much for Albert. In 1928 he collapsed with such severe heart trouble that it took him almost a year to recover.

Food was scarce in Germany after World War I. Children gathered at street kitchens for food handouts. To help out, Albert insisted on being paid when he was photographed, then donated the money to feed the starving children.

Elsa came with Albert on his first trip to the United States in 1921. Everywhere Albert went people wanted to interview him and talk to him.

"Imagination is more important than knowledge."
— Albert

The architect of the Einstein Tower in Potsdam, Germany, wanted its design to be as revolutionary as Albert's ideas.

Albert won a Nobel prize for physics, not for his theories on relativity, but for his work in 1905 on the quantum theory of light. Some physicists still didn't accept Albert's theory of relativity.

Good-bye Germany

Adolph Hitler, leader of the Nazi party, became dictator of Germany in 1933. Before World War II was over, he'd be responsible for the death of at least six million Jews. Albert helped more than 200 Jewish refugees escape to the United States.

"Organized power can be opposed only by organized power. Much as I regret this, there is no other way."
— Albert

By the late 1920s, the Nazi party was becoming more powerful in Germany, and Albert was worried. The Nazis hated Jews, and they also wanted to extend their power into other countries. Albert knew this meant war. He also was aware that he was at risk — the Nazis were suspicious of his peace work, and he was Jewish.

When Albert left Germany in late 1932 to visit the United States, he knew he would never return. A few weeks later, he and Elsa learned that the Nazis had taken over Germany. Their summer home near Berlin was wrecked. The next summer, Albert lectured in Europe, but he and Elsa soon realized they were in danger and must leave.

Albert had already agreed to become a professor at the new Institute of Advanced Study at Princeton University in New Jersey. He and Elsa sailed to New York in October 1933, but they slipped off the boat before its final stop to avoid the crowds waiting to greet them.

Once settled in Princeton, Albert was again consumed by his study of physics. That made him absentminded. One day the university office got a call from a man asking for directions to Albert's house. When the clerk wouldn't tell him, the man sighed, "This *is* Albert Einstein. I got lost walking home ..."

The quantum theory occupied Albert's mind now. This theory describes the tiny particles that make up atoms, such as protons, neutrons and electrons, and how they move randomly in waves. Albert didn't think the theory was complete, but other scientists, including Nobel prize winner Niels Bohr, accepted it as it was. Albert disagreed with his good friend Niels and kept working on his own version of it.

Working with physicists Boris Podolsky and Nathan Rosen, Albert also predicted some strange consequences of the quantum theory. The men argued that objects that are very far apart can still affect each other. This is now known as the EPR paradox (the name comes from the initials of the three physicists' last names) and may some day lead to teleportation.

The threat of war in Europe worried Albert more and more. The Nazis even made him change his mind about peace — he now felt that they were so evil that the only way to stop them was to fight. Still, Albert was deeply saddened when, in 1939, World War II broke out. His theories would help bring the war to an end, but in a way he never imagined.

Albert's books and many others written by Jews were judged by the Nazis to be "un-German" and were burned on huge bonfires.

Albert's white, wooden house in Princeton had a big backyard.

NEW YORK STATE

New York City

Princeton

NEW JERSEY

In 1933 Albert sailed from Europe to New York City. Princeton, New Jersey, where he lived for more than 20 years, is about 80 km (50 mi.) to the southwest.

I liked to look out over the gardens while I played my violin.

Albert and Elsa were welcomed by Hopi living near the Grand Canyon, Arizona, in 1931. They gave Albert a headdress and called him "the Great Relative."

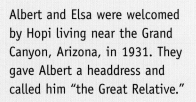

Atom bomb!

The outbreak of World War II horrified Albert, but he was even more appalled to hear that German scientists were working on an atom bomb. In the late 1930s, physicists in Europe had discovered that it was possible to split the nucleus (central core) of an uranium atom. This could lead to an enormous release of energy — Albert's $E = mc^2$ equation told exactly how much. An atom bomb made this way could destroy a whole city.

Albert had to do something, fast. If the Nazis had such a powerful weapon, they could take over the world. In 1939, encouraged by other physicists, he wrote to American President Franklin D. Roosevelt and urged the United States to build its own atom bomb. Roosevelt agreed and launched the Manhattan Project. Manhattan is the part of New York City where people first gathered to do research into making an atom bomb. But most of the Project's work was done secretly in the desert, at Los Alamos, New Mexico.

Since Albert had worked out the equation describing how much energy splitting an atom released, you'd think he'd be part of the Manhattan Project. But he didn't have the know-how to work on constructing an atom bomb because he wasn't a nuclear physicist. And the U.S. government felt he was too outspoken to be trusted with secrets.

The more Albert thought about how destructive an atom bomb would be, the more it frightened him. As well, the war with Germany was almost over, so there was no need for such a terrible weapon, Albert felt. In 1945 he wrote a second letter to President Roosevelt warning what could happen if an atom bomb were ever used. But Roosevelt died before he read Albert's letter. The Manhattan Project kept going.

Albert didn't know that the United States had successfully made an atom bomb until he heard on the radio that one had been dropped on Japan on August 6, 1945. Almost 200 000 people were injured or killed in the cities of Hiroshima and, three days later, Nagasaki. The Japanese surrendered and World War II was finally over.

When Albert heard how people suffered in Japan because of the bombs, he was devastated. "I could burn my fingers that I wrote that first letter to President Roosevelt" urging the United States to create an atom bomb, he said. Albert called the letter "the greatest mistake of my life." From then on, Albert worked harder than ever for world peace.

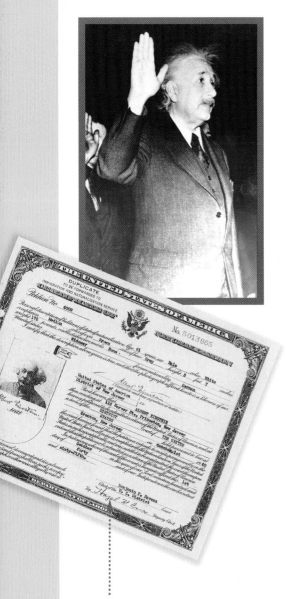

In 1940 Albert became an American citizen and pledged the oath of allegiance to his new country.

"Shall we put an end to the human race or shall mankind renounce war? People will not face this alternative because it is so difficult to abolish war." — Albert

J. Robert Oppenheimer (right) was in charge of the Manhattan Project that created the atom bomb. He admired Albert's sense of humor and kindness.

I later came to wish I'd never written this letter to the President.

Here's the first letter Albert wrote to American President Roosevelt.

Albert Einstein
Old Grove Rd.
Nassau Point
Peconic, Long Island

August 2nd, 1939

.D. Roosevelt,
resident of the United States,
white House
Washington, D.C.

Sir:

Some recent work by E.Fermi and L. Szilard, which has be̶̶n̶com-
municated to me in manuscript, leads me to expect that the element ur̶
ium may be turned into a new and important source of energy in the immediate future. Certain aspects of the situation which has arisen seem
to call for watchfulness and, if necessary, quick action on the part
of the Administration. I believe therefore that it is my duty to bring
to your attention the following facts and recommendations:

In the course of the last four months it has been made probable -
the work of Joliot in France as well as Fermi and Szilard in
may become possible to set up a nuclear chain reaction
by which vast amounts of power and large quant-
would be generated. Now it appears
the immediate future.
struction of bombs,

Atom bombs destroy by generating searing heat and winds many times stronger than hurricanes. They also cause intense radiation that injures or kills people.

Last questions

When Albert was asked to become Israel's president he said, "I am deeply moved by the offer of Israel. And at once saddened and ashamed that I cannot accept it." (The blue and white of the Israeli flag, above, symbolize purity and spirituality.)

This is where Albert spent years thinking about the relationship between the main forces of nature. Although he didn't succeed, he said, "At least I know 99 ways that do not work."

After the war Albert campaigned hard for the end of atomic weapons. He also supported the United Nations and spoke out about the rights of black people and other minorities. But physics still absorbed most of his attention. He continued to work on the unified field theory to connect the theories of electromagnetism and gravity.

Albert traveled less and less as he got older. His wife Elsa had died in 1936, and now he lived with her daughter, Margot, his sister, Maja, and secretary, Helen Dukas. Hans Albert, his elder son, was an engineering professor in California and a world expert on the transport of silt and sediment. He visited his father several times. Eduard, Albert's other son, was mentally ill and lived in an institution in Switzerland. The last time Albert ever saw him was in 1934.

In 1945 Albert retired from the Institute for Advanced Study. He was sick a lot because he'd developed an aneurysm in his stomach. That means the walls of a blood vessel had weakened and expanded. Doctors warned him that his heart was also weak, but he wouldn't stop working.

When Israel needed a new president in 1952, the country's prime minister decided to ask the most famous and brilliant Jewish person in the world. Albert was honored but had to say no — he was aware that he was too blunt and didn't always get along with people. He was more comfortable in the world of science.

On Wednesday, April 13, 1955, Albert's aneurysm burst. He knew he was dying, but asked for his glasses to be brought to his hospital room and kept working. Albert Einstein died early on the morning of April 18. His last words were in German. The nurse who was with him didn't speak German, so no one knows what he said. Beside his bed was a paper covered with unfinished calculations.

Albert didn't see himself as a hero and didn't want a big tombstone when he died. He was cremated and his ashes scattered secretly. He had also asked that his house in Princeton not be turned into a museum.

Albert solved problems that had puzzled physicists for 200 years. It will take much longer than that before science understands the full meaning of his work.

This statue of Albert is in Washington, D.C., but there are memorials to him all over the world. *Time* magazine also named him the Person of the Century for the last century.

Even as an old man Albert thought more about the future than about the past. He tried to make the world a safer, more peaceful place.

"One thing I have learned in a long life: that all our science, measured against reality, is primitive and childlike — and yet it is the most precious thing we have."
— Albert

Newspapers everywhere carried the news that the world's most famous scientist was dead.

ATTACK ON WHITE RULE

NTO DAILY STAR

EINSTEIN IS DEAD

METRO EDITION

Life and physics since Albert

"The important thing is not to stop questioning."
— Albert

Albert won many awards and even had a crater on the Moon and a new kind of atom (einsteinium) named after him.

For a long time people wondered what made Albert a genius. So Albert asked that his brain be available for research after he died. Almost 50 years after his death, doctors at McMaster University in Hamilton, Ontario, discovered that there were only a few differences between Albert's brain and the average brain.

Albert's brain was missing a small wrinkle that many people have. The areas on either side are a bit bigger, and those are the regions that work on math and imaging. Also, the groove that runs from front to back in most people's brains didn't extend all the way in Albert's. This may have helped the nerve cells there connect and work together better.

Thanks to Albert and his amazing brain, we have nuclear power, radiation therapy to treat cancer and gamma ray scans to check out your bones — they're all based on Albert's famous $E = mc^2$ equation. Albert's work on the quantum theory of light has led to fluorescent lights, automatic doors, lasers and more.

Albert's general theory of relativity also helped astronomers discover pulsars (a kind of star that gives off pulses of radiation) and quasars (star-like objects that are very far away). This theory also led, in 1971, to the discovery of black holes, regions in space with such strong gravity that no objects or light can escape. The big bang theory about the origin of the universe is also based on his theory.

Science is still trying to catch up with Albert. In the fall of 2002, NASA launched its *Gravity Probe B* to test two new important predictions from Albert's general theory of relativity.

The world learned more than just a new way of looking at the universe from Albert. He also showed how important creativity and imagination are. Through hard work and creative thinking, Albert Einstein found answers that forever changed people's understanding of the world.

Since the first atom bomb was created using Albert's $E = mc^2$ equation, many countries have built these powerful bombs. The Doomsday Clock is a worldwide symbol of atomic danger — the closer the hands are to midnight, the closer the world is to destruction by atom bombs.

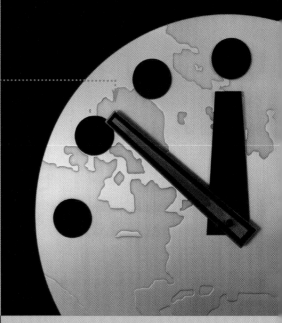

Albert's brain weighed about the same as the average man's, but the portion that deals with visualizing and mathematical thinking was 15 percent wider.

Now astronomers know that many spiral galaxies have a black hole at their centers, just as Albert predicted.

Science fiction writers and artists are inspired by Albert's work to think differently about our world and other distant worlds.

Albert's life at a glance

1879   March 14 — Albert Einstein born in Ulm, Germany

1880   June 21 — The Einstein family moves to Munich, Germany

1881   November 18 — Albert's sister, Maria (he called her Maja), is born

1894   June — The Einsteins move to Milan, Italy, but Albert stays in Munich

December 29 — Albert drops out of school and joins his family in Milan

1895   Albert fails the entry exam for the Swiss Federal Institute of Technology in Zurich, Switzerland, and goes back to school for a year

1896   January 28 — Albert officially gives up his German citizenship to avoid having to join the army

October — Albert begins studying at the Swiss Federal Institute of Technology. He graduates in 1900 as a math teacher.

1901   February 21 — Albert officially becomes a Swiss citizen

May–July — Albert works as a teacher at a private school and as a temporary teacher

1902   January — Albert's daughter, Lieserl, is born

June 16 — Albert is hired as a patent officer in Bern, Switzerland

1903   January 6 — Albert and Mileva are married in Bern

April — Albert forms Olympia Academy with two friends

1904   May 14 — Albert's first son, Hans Albert, is born

1905   Albert publishes four papers that change the world of physics. His papers include the "Special Theory of Relativity."

1906   January 15 — Albert receives his doctorate from the University of Zurich

1908   February 28 — Albert takes a very junior teaching position at Bern University

1909   May 7 — Albert is appointed professor of theoretical physics at University of Zurich

1910   July 28 — Albert's second son, Eduard, is born

1911   Albert becomes a full professor at Karl-Ferdinand University in Prague

He attends the first Solvay Congress

1912   January 30 — Albert is appointed professor at the Zurich Polytechnic

1913   December 7 — Albert accepts a position as professor at the University of Berlin

1914   World War I breaks out

June — Albert and Mileva separate. She returns to Zurich with their sons.

1915   November — Albert signs a "Manifesto to the Europeans" explaining his pacifist feelings

1916   Albert publishes a paper proposing the final version of his general theory of relativity. He is elected president of the German Physical Society.

1917   October 1 — The Kaiser Wilhelm Institute for Physics in Berlin opens with Albert as director

1918   World War I ends

1919   Albert obtains a divorce and marries his cousin Elsa Löwenthal

November 6 — A solar eclipse lets British astronomers confirm the general theory of relativity. Albert becomes world famous.

1920   Albert given a top award from France, the *Ordre pour la Merité*

1921   April–May — Albert visits the United States for the first time

1922   Albert works on the unified field theory

October — Albert tours Japan, Hong Kong, Singapore, Palestine and Spain

November — Albert wins the Nobel prize for his work on the quantum theory of light

1924   The Einstein Institute opens in Potsdam, Germany

1925   Albert predicts the existence of Bose-Einstein condensates

Albert tours South America

Albert is given the Copley Medal from the Royal Society, a famous organization of leading British scientists, and the gold medal of the Royal Astronomical Society of London

1928   Albert suffers from heart trouble

1929   Albert wins the Max Planck Medal, a major physics prize

1932   Albert leaves Germany and never returns

August — Albert is appointed a professor at the Institute of Advanced Study in Princeton

1933   The Nazis burn all of Albert's papers in Germany

October 17 — Albert and Elsa move to the United States

1935   Albert and two co-workers write a paper about the EPR paradox. This is Albert's last great paper and, after being ignored for many years, it is now having a huge influence on science.

1936   December 20 — Elsa Einstein dies in Princeton, New Jersey

1939   World War II breaks out

August 2 — Albert writes to American President Roosevelt warning him that German scientists are working on an atom bomb

1940   October 1 — Albert becomes an American citizen

1945   Atom bombs are dropped on Hiroshima and Nagasaki. World War II ends.

1948   Albert publishes his last attempt at a unified field theory

1951   Maja, Albert's sister, dies

1952   November — Albert is offered the presidency of Israel but turns it down

1955   April 18 — Albert dies in Princeton, New Jersey

Visit Albert

Einstein-Haus, Kramgasse 49, CH-3000 BERN 8, Switzerland

Albert lived here from 1902 to 1909 and always said this was when he was happiest and got the most work done. He was living here in 1905 when he published his physics papers that changed the world.

Albert Einstein Memorial, National Academy of Sciences, Washington, D.C.

This huge statue — it weighs 4 tn (tons) — is in the southwest corner of the Academy's grounds. Turn to page 27 to see it. The papers in Albert's hand show some of his work on his theory of general relativity, his theory $E = mc^2$ and the quantum theory.

112 Mercer Street, Princeton University, New Jersey

You can't tour the house where Albert lived in Princeton from 1935 to 1955, but you can drive by it.

Einstein Tower, Potsdam, Germany

Originally built to hold Albert's astronomy lab, this tower is still used for research about the Sun. You can take a look at the tower on page 21.

There are statues and memorials of me all over the world. These are just a few of them.

Index